Black Print
Vol. I

ANONYMITY

Copyright © 2020 Anonymity The Poet.
All rights reserved. This book or any portion thereof may not be reproduced or used in any manner whatsoever without the express written permission of the publisher except for the use of brief quotations in a book review.

Printed by Ingramspark Inc. in the United States of America

First printing edition 2020.

Publisher
Anonymity
PO Box 66046 TOWN CENTRE
PICKERING ON L1V 6P7

www.anonymitywords.com

The Sun gives life to Earth
it cannot exist alone
The very same way
She gives life to man

How can someone tell you how to feel
as if they have seen pain through your eyes
they can't see the beauty behind the woman
past the curves and the unmatched style

what is perceived isn't necessarily what is shown
and the truth of what is seen isn't always known
subjected to all manner of emotion
some positive often a negative notion

can you say majesty without woman
some consider her in lieu of man
but purposeful ignorance is a sin

seen but not seen amongst a myriad of others
overlooked until they are forced
to do more than is required
to be noticed and unintentionally desired

how many people can relate
to a life of constant debate
of whether your hurt is abundant
or your love is enough

I'm wondering if he looks at you
the way you look at him
if focus is love why isn't his attention
pointed at you
are priorities where they are suppose to be?
or does the temptation
of elsewhere disrupt the frequency
How many men look at you?
vying for his coveted position in your life
space is limited and there's room for only one
sitting in between tear drops
letting attachment drain your smile away

Your touch takes him places

hes never dreamed of

fantasy lays asleep in bed with reality

the two are one and the two are separate

is there anywhere else

that dreams come to sleep

or does happiness only exist in your arms

Dedicated to your dreams
your life and your love
the heat they feel
is the fire in your heart

The scariest thing about you

is that you deserve more

than mortal men can give

All the ways that love exists
can be learned from watching you
you wrote the love languages
even though
you taught him what he knows
he doesn't know
everything that you do

Have any kisses ever

scattered the butterflies in a stomach

the way yours can

do lips have the power to

water the mouth at their thought

the way yours do

maybe that's why it's so easy

to be obsessed with you

I never believed in love at first sight
until you proved that life imitates art
now you're compared to
the most romantic stories
and the most remote places
because you are love
and you can only be found
if you travel far enough

What felt like countless years
turned out to be just short of a lifetime
of a together that ended in your youth
now he dies everyday without rest
you were the life in him
and now he chokes on your memory
as your absence exposed
his emotions mortality
now it's clear that man can't live
without love

I think the best thing about you

is when the words "I love you"

part your lips

the definition of giving love

the way that we are never worthy

of Gods grace

I don't know anyone worthy

of hearing you say those words

Life in your presence

is always a little better

save for the pride

that won't let someone admit

that you've taken them to

a different place

I see you inside

and laugh at the best of times

that only come from these moments

ones that can't be imagined

hoping forever isn't a lie

and some things do last

I need it all the time

a taste is too much of a tease

floating in the land of milk and honey

only to wake up

in your room desperate for a drink

from the bottle of water you keep

on your night stand

SIA

Understanding is only the beginning
can they feel what you've been through?
do they see your smile through it all
they've never read your story
they only see a cute face and small waist
and they forget that sometimes
you get tired of being strong.

Your love wasn't meant for men
who can't hold the sun
in their hands
without getting burnt

It belongs to men who look up at the moon
and bask in how it lights up the night sky

Peace rests in your voice

shared with every word you speak

I can't believe it was born

out of chaos

Your mother should have named you ambition

in what meaning does a word exist

only in your name does ambition have meaning

You live by the standards
you hold in your heart
climbing the ladder to reach them,
is not
a task to be picked up on a Sunday afternoon

better to lay alone
than to lay down
with a partner
in a place you left long ago

can peaks be reached without drowning
in dedication,
can you be reached without
swimming in obsession

Flawed in your understanding
only with the best intentions
do your actions come across
as hurtful
you love differently
more completely
even more intensely
but not the way
they need to feel love
pushed away in desperation
because there is no discerning
only a daze
and in the end a parting

Closest to perfections peak
mentally exceeding
physically intimidating
spiritually enlightened
there aren't many men
who fit in your category
that's what makes it better
humility is your name sake
and deserving your birth right

looking down at the clouds

and up at the sky

swelling in pride at the thought

of a love that connects

to the heart

and relaxes the mind

in its untreated state

how much better

will it be

when its purified

when it can be called

true love

Waxing and waning

like the tides of the oceans

your love burns hot

on the coldest days

and freezes over

when the sun comes out

surrendering to temporary feelings

regretting permanent decisions

it all comes from fear

sabotaging your love

for a life you may not want

Living in a world of idealism

I've watched you

walk back into rooms

you should have left ages ago

all because you dream

in a different hue

shame on you for being fooled

too many times

with an air of hope

you reject the reality of

the man you won't let go

Why can he only see you as an object?
to be used, thrown away and ridiculed
too loving to refuse
demands that you were once unsure of
but now you know better
that yours is more important
than his desire to take away your life

How many ways
can they misunderstand
the direction of the tides, the ones
that pull you under in the blink of an eye
the expectations of a woman
overwhelm the ill prepared
and swallow the careless

Caution thrown to the wind

in favour of solitude

better to be alone

than to fall

for companies misery

I hate the lies you tell
whispered in my ear
stories about forever
attention given to the weather
it can fall on anyones shoulders
burdened with love
that should have been mine
taken to places
we should have went together
smiles taken by the unearned

Eyes from everywhere looking in
life on display
in a world without haven

where can she go
where judgement
doesn't break the nights rest

is self love not enough
in the face of critique
will her best ever be
enough for a world
where enough is never enough

How much more of yourself

can you give away

to the wolves

ravaging what's left of you

taking the heart out of your chest

only to leave you barren

in your own body

a shell of a woman

with nowhere to go

Can I hold you close

the void is only in the mind

while Umoja is alive

in the heart

forgetting what it means

to be and be loved

now just the void

and drifting

Orbiting as close

to the stars

as a you can get

The word that burns a hole
in your mind is focus
destroyed from within
by melancholic thoughts
dug up from the fears of
external results that may
or may not exist anywhere
but in your mind they are more real
than the eyes in your head
that see possibilities
competition the root
produced and manufactured
in places where success is mirrored
by insecurity in a partner
who can't see teamwork
through the dream

Always a little bit of yesterday

in your mind

the what ifs and the could haves

even worse when

you catch their eye in a place

that you never expected

to bump heads

just to see them with

the next one who isn't you

So much purity in woman
actions performed with the heart
only explained by gratitude
her last is freely given
only Jesus could give more
so willingly
with him in mind
she has poured out all she has
two pennies placed atop
a bag full of gold
to a love given back to her
in full from a man
only God could assign her

How do you paint a Goddess
with a brush as delicate as the dove
in dark colours and shades
the colours of fire, passion and love
an all encompassing hue that never fades

She sits in the presence of peace
as onlookers stare in awe
in a room full of women she is the center piece
her energy demands attention as if it were natures law

The type of woman who inspires the inspiring
for her nothing more than a thoughtless task
they find themselves unintentionally admiring
drawn to the vision of the sun to bask

You nurture

beyond what the eyes can see

picking up the pieces

of hearts you didn't hurt

maybe that's why

they fall for you so quickly

thinking you've picked up their affections

when really

you're just tired of being around

broken men who forgot how to love

Willing to love, and get lost
in the vulnerability of it all
where others may call you crazy
you're the only one
who is truly living a life fulfilled
with your heart open, but wise
and your vision clear but hopeful
you've found the perfect place to live
in the moment.

You hold on tighter than the average

but once you let go

nothing can make you look back

because you love yourself enough

to not turn mistakes into habits

They knock at your door

with a hand full of apologies

but nothing new on their lips

because they've tasted your love

and now

they're going through withdrawals

You attract what you want
and get what you need
magnetic personality
causes silver and gold
to be drawn in
by your you

What heights can't be reached
by a woman with a vision
the glass ceiling is only a concept
that is shattered by all your power

To be told you are perfect

is an insult within itself

why strive for perfection

when you can live in the euphoria

of constantly growing

more beautiful

in mind body and spirit

Reaching for what's considered
impossible
but for you
it is just the inevitable
life mixed in with goals
and nothing can stop
your climb

*Waking up to your smile
is glass of wine in your hand
and the sun on your skin*

They come crawling back
and are left staring at you
through a screen
the closest he will ever
get to you again

Powerful words fall from your lips
influencing lives in each breathe you take
breathing life into man, love and family

These men follow you

without knowing

what it means to hold you close

they see who you are, and desire it

but they can't figure out

how to capture your heart

the man who steals it

would be as Samson to men

but valentine to your heart

You hold the burden of loyalty
closer to your heart than most
defining faithfulness
in the face of temptations kiss
mouths speak rumours
steeped in misconception
where one may think
you are named for another
sirens sing to the waters
calling the waves
to flow over your mind
but you don't swim
in confusions currents
shattering efforts
to drown you
in self doubt

Family holds the most power
in the struggle to remain sane
how do you fight against life
when you can only exist in it
leaving your mind out of it
leading with your heart
you'll be an ancestor one day
and give the family
to your loves and loved ones

Driving and disconnecting
musical therapy
at unbelievable speeds
you can't hear any words
over the sound of the melody
it's not enough to let go
sometimes you need to be alone
peace requires isolation
and growth requires peace
the goal to be one more
than yesterday
as you work your way
down the highway

Can mistakes be reversed

when the past comes calling

who will be there

to put it back on the shelf

it was never meant to wake up

and now it rises in the morning

focused while walking through

anxieties desert sands

the air chokes most

you're a woman who was born

to live in the heat

and grow in the fire

the hard times are draining

you don't show pain

to the takers

and exude love

to the deservers

who said hard times

were meant to destroy

when difficulty

creates powerful women

Why can't they stay away
friends and family alike
why is your heart so giving
and your mind so fulfilling
does love have limits
or do you forgive
like Gods grace eternal
angelic qualities
are they the factor
the magnet
that keeps you
in the mind and presence
of loved ones
and ones who wish
to be loved

Born again too many times

to the same mistake

love and insanity creating

the same efforts

but different results

beauty in the struggle

you love the turns it takes

and

the mistakes it makes

you've been away for some time

but you come back

to be born again

to the same love and insanity

that keeps you smiling

So far away from home
just in your mind do you
feel like a foreigner

where do you start
when you have purpose
but fear
eats away at progress

lost in the day time
and restless at night
the path is cleared
by steps
not looks and thoughts

You've been living in your head
for so long
anyone who wants to join you
has to dive into your depths
and speak the language
of your mind
you've been fluent in solitude
for much longer than
you would like
but you can't communicate
with someone who only
speaks in past tense

You wear your heart
where your head should be
and love your way through logic
that might be why
your love paints murals
across the coldest stone walls
you choose water colours
because they wash off easiest
you can't stay too long
in places without warmth

All that love is seen,

but goes unnoticed

and you're tired

of trying to show it

wrapped up in the wiles

of what companionship means

to a woman who knows what she wants

and men who barely

 know who they are

How can your mind feel again
when freedom is so out of your reach
given a blessing in a package
that many consider baggage
by someone who wasn't as graceful
and chained you to him
with no intention of letting go
disguised as freddy at night
to kill the dreams of love again

Encased in gold 24 karats

tongue dripping with silver

the atmosphere

sweetly incensed

your every step gifted to

loves definition

a meaning reborn

in your image

affordable only to

those with emotions

laid bare

Embracing the mortality of love

two hearts on life support

tied together by arithmetic

speaking a common language

in different dialects

if only walking away

was as easy

as laying down together

The way you tease with your eyes

and capture with your smile

almost hypnotic

the way you make my mind go blank

and bring me out of a shell

that I never knew was there

your powers are mesmerizing

Changing the meaning

of forgiveness

you give grace

in ways

second only to God

Giving up slowly each day
this fake love isn't enough
to satisfy the hunger in your belly
how many of them
are willing to really know you
to see you naked in all your clothing
to get to the bottom of vulnerability
who can dig through your you
to find you

beauty born in physical form
personified by lifes theme

sun kissed and glowing
conceived by purpose

and in the 9th month
ready to give the world
your gift

How do you paint her
created in hues of darkness
with flecks of gold and
the softest touches of lavender
built like the pyramids
God the architect
Made of passion
Persistence the mortar
With love at the core
swirling colours
beauties definition malleable
in the face of different faces
falling in love is the expectant
and admiration the intoxicant
she does not exist for your pleasure
but she brings untold amounts
that a life without her lacks

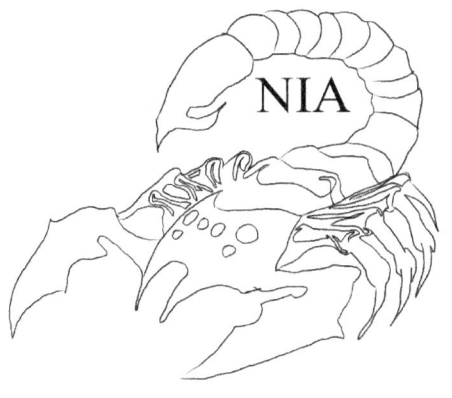

Growing up too fast
beautiful little island girl
who chose the world
even when it didn't choose her
you leave pieces of your heart
everywhere you go
with men who never wanted it
once the size of a country
able to house a nation
now you can't tell it apart
from the grains of sand
on a beach

Beautiful was coined with you in mind

God practicing his creation

and perfecting his craft

the final product held more meaning

than one thousand failures

if only you saw yourself through

the eyes of your maker

words would run down your skin

like water

instead of weighing you down

like anxiety

How many of your peers
envy the ease of your flow
you make everything
look as simple as
watching the sun rise
beauty in the smile
you wear
in the face of jealousy
spinning a tale of effort
of never giving up

Waiting for love in a place
where trust doesn't exist
giving your self away
to loneliness
with every touch
sleeping in regret
with each kiss
running out of places to hide
sanctum doesn't exist
for failed love and broken hearts
mistakes are only made once
now you're just choosing
to dive into the pain

Reaching out to feel
be seen and felt
questioning decisions
with indecision
while confidence
dies in favour of doubt
is surety so foreign
that it only thrives
across the ocean
under a different sky
can being touched
feel sacred again
or does tradition die
with conception

Confusion as a character trait
because the mind is never still
reflections are only seen
when the ripples are absent
how can you hear your own voice
if you can't be silent enough
to hear it speak its language
truth its native tongue
It's directed geniuses
to the immortality
you only hear about in stories

Days of hurt stretched into weeks
then months and longer still to years
living far away
the past still appears
in everything you do
and every word you say
seemingly like twins in appearance
but something you'd rather leave behind
the pain is the steel chain
that keeps you bound to yesterday
something you feel just to misunderstand
what you understand about the way you feel
visions of the future will only ever be dreams
if images of the past are recurring nightmares

So much beauty lost
in a self deprecating tongue

power lives in the mind
and vision of the woman

her weakness takes over
with words of self hate
anger and confusion

Tired of the late night phone calls
depending on anyones conversation
desperate enough to hear any voice
even ones that shouldn't be graced
with the sounds of yours

selling your time for a sprinkle of love
because you've lost sight
of understanding
that you are love
that you are the supplier
of what life is made of

So much in one woman
written in loves language
Indiscernible from her stare

Focus and love
twins

rarely recognized together
Deepest dedication

To all that she embodies
obsession to all that she is

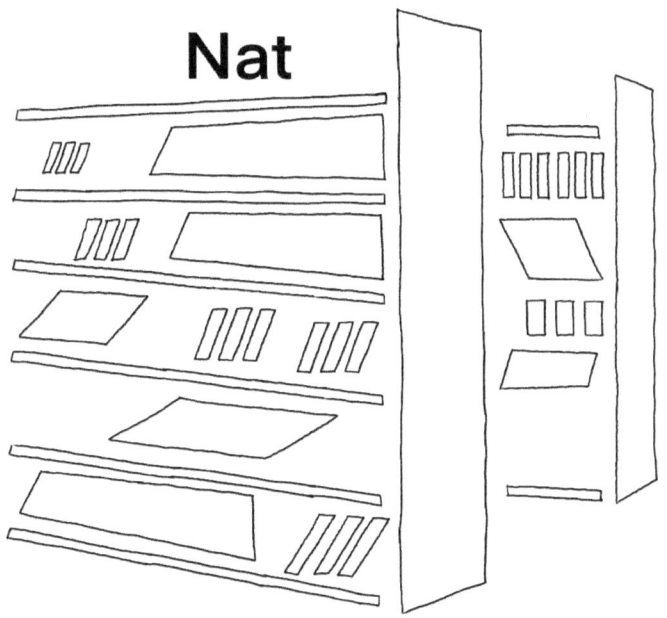

Without you there will never be another

that fills him up to overflowing

with confidence and happiness

The many efforts to

create a lasting legacy

are plagued with challenges

you want your last name

to live on long after

you've passed away

even though you are afraid

you possess courage

only God can instill

so success is your reward

Past familiarity on the way
to much more
residing in the same place
at different times
makes companionship harder
than staring into the sun
speaking words of revelry
in the others absence
you've looked into
 one anothers eyes
and saw the passion
that lives there
a stomach full of nerves
and a mind full of fear
there isn't enough room
in one body
for butterflies and regret

You make him feel alive
like the melting of the snow
and the emergence of spring
you bring out the flowers
in hearts all around you
a ray of sunshine is too cliché
of a comparison
you are more like
the invention of ice cream
in 40 degree weather

Just like the flower
that looks up at the moon
and asks where the sun has gone
so have you sparked inspiration
into minds and hearts
in the footprints left behind
meeting isn't left up to fate
God decides whose lives
are changed by your love

Born whole and complete
another half isn't what you seek
two wholes together made perfect
is the desire of the content
what more can someone add
to your finished self
you rather someone share
their full self with you
than to try to add
to your whole

Do two empty roads ever
intertwine the way yours have
connecting the right moments
always the wrong time
just long enough to know
what you want
never long enough to have it
at times we let God lead us back
to the path he designed for us
and it inevitably ends
at the same place as yours

Love as rare as a black rose
with the same meaning as red
but feels like yellow
and as warm as the July sun
only travelling so far to find you
enduring the harshest climb
over mountains of failed amour
do you come to appreciate
how unique the black rose is

The thought of without you
is social anxiety and first day jitters
mixed with the fear of failure

While being lost in a strange city
in the middle of the night

I want to always be confident
and secure
so I need you next to me

So we can get found
for the first time

in foreign countries
like two residents
in every place we are together

How brave is your every action
where you have to be strong
one day you hope that
you don't have to be strong alone
anymore

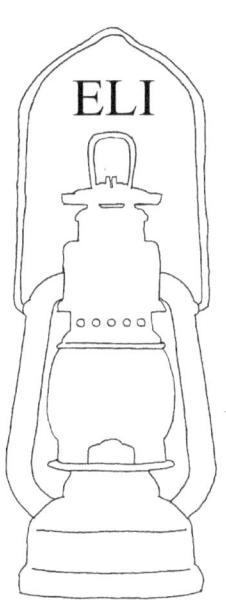

Stuck in perpetual struggle

of doing a little too much

and receiving too little in return

your heart cracks at each encounter

with the ungrateful

you don't know how

 to stop hurting yourself

how to stop loving

no one taught you how to turn it off

stuck in this mode you grew up in

without ever taking a break for yourself

You've been placing others before you
since the conception of time itself
selflessness is heavy at times
a gift of recurring generosity
your super power
sprinkled in the hearts
of the few and the chosen
in the midst of a world
where selfishness is a key ingredient
to existence and surviving
you found a way to thrive
while giving your all
to everyone around you

Betrayal is your lifes theme

always a receiver of disappointment

sometimes expectations

were never meant to exist in that relationship

your heart is strong in the face of new deception

you will never be destroyed

by another persons weaknesses

that is your power

almost super

when weighed against the trials

of a harsh world

How you adore the simplicity of life
made in the image of a single white rose
the beauty of purity and elegance
for you
it adds no meaning
to be included in the bouquet
you see it in no other way
than the littlest of things
that bring endless smiles to your face
appreciation is an expensive thought
that a woman like you can afford
to buy 31 times a month

Surviving in this world for too long
in the eye of a storm
of indecision of what to do next
thoughts flowing by like a river
your decision to enter the water
only gets harder as more time passes by
the currents get fiercer and fear
seems to occupy the waters depths
how can you move forward
if you aren't willing to get your feet wet
something is only new for a short time
while familiarity lasts forever

The days start to blur

mixing together in a perpetual pattern

of eat sleep and die at the end of a long day

to be resurrected

by necessity the next morning

your purpose is one decision away

the bravery to make the choice

to become the manifestation

you are capable of being

Just once you want to be proven wrong
for all your past experiences to be nullified
to fall away in the presence of real love
it seems like the end is always written
before the journey even starts
and you've read the same ending
enough times to fill a calendar

Born from the offspring

of traumas descendants

the line continues

into the next generation

the pain passed down brushed off

as hereditary and familial norms

so when you see it

and feel it

you embrace it

because it's all you've ever known

fed knowledge that coincides

with its justification

to wake up one day

not realizing you've been crying inside

everyday

since you were a child

It is a wonder how

you continue to feel

when you should be numb

tragedy stricken

time and time again

and still loving as hard

as a toddler at the sight of

her loving parents

some may think you are naïve

that you haven't learned from the past

but the choice to love fully

while carrying the lessons of the night before

is a better way to live your life

than living in the tragedies of yesterday

The most admirable thing
you've done
is hold on all this time
trying too hard for too long
absent appreciations smiling face
to make everything seem worth it
you give your own meaning to struggle
where most will never understand
you are the bravest in the face
of the dark tunnel that is your path
with your eyes fixed firmly
at the light at the end

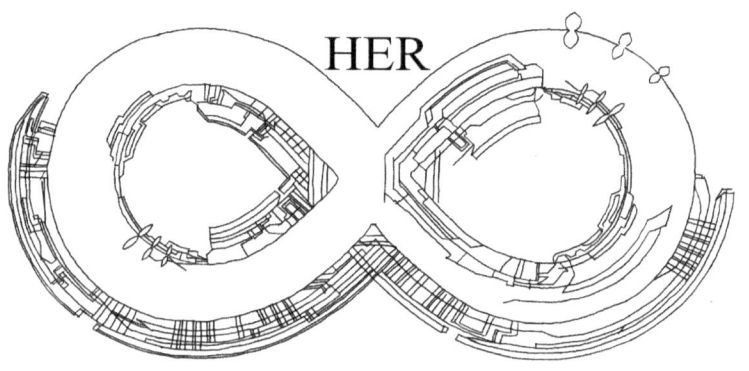

Many of us see the face of her
pain masked with smiles
and the phrase "I'm fine"
often falls from her lips at reflex
like rain from the sky
tear drops form
in the comfort of solitude
her feelings are hidden
because in most cases
nobody cares

Her invincibility is a mystery

broken at every turn

but she moves forward

and gains even more

than she possessed before

Architect and designer of loves ecstasy
was your heart ever so full
until she showed you what it means to be filled
there is a reason you can't let go
feelings were so foreign before your meeting
with shallow examples of love
that were never real in the face of her
she took you to places
opened up your world
showed you the you in you
that you didn't know was missing

It can seem like a fairytale

to those who lay eyes on her

the type of energy she brings

something only heard of in forgotten stories

retold a thousand times

 in a thousand beautiful ways

like the odyssey or the Iliad

you can only understand if you are there to see

who she really is

all the feelings she creates

is a side effect

of a presence she embodies

so intentionally

not for you

but for her own sanity

Loves teacher and its first student
she was born special
strong enough to hold
your splintering world together
delicate enough to feel all your pain
understanding enough to know
where all you hurt comes from

There is a goddess in her

one that sleeps in her heart

but is alive in her eyes

to look into her

will age a man ten years

gaining wisdom

that a boy could never comprehend

I hope you love her mother

as much as you love her

without her Matriarch

she wouldn't be

the blessing you cherish

and the one

other men wish they had

How many times have you
taken her for granted
and broken her heart
falling on your knees
begging her to stay
her grace is close to Gods
but she must love herself
a little bit more
than she loves you

All her confidence
misinterpreted as attitude
purposely
to save your ego
and keep your pride intact

She refuses with her all
to take the damage
you are trying to deal
in her life

While you yearn for other women
she stays loyal to you
at the same time
other men look at her
and tell her how amazing she is
I hope you appreciate her
before she lets some one else
do what you were suppose to

Have you ever wondered
where she came from
How was she able
to add so much to a life
you thought was enough
and leave you empty
in her absence

The 8th wonder of the world
Gods gift to man
he doesn't know her real value
she teaches love and grace
takes on the worlds pain and tears

souls are sold to taste her lips
even just once is
enough to need rehabilitation
I don't want to exist
in places she doesn't want to be

I've learned to hold onto what is important

Special Thanks

To the amazing women
who inspired this collection of poems

www.ingramcontent.com/pod-product-compliance
Lightning Source LLC
Chambersburg PA
CBHW072204100526
44589CB00015B/2355